flüchtigen Augenblicke

ein Tupfer Sonnenlicht

die Tiefe des Gartens in Licht und Schatten

Gräser im Gegenlicht

Schindeln im kurzen Moment des Streiflichts

goldener Schimmer des Nachmittags Winterlicht

das Flimmern des reflekting Pools

Wasser: als Spiegel des Himmels, das flüchtige

Feuerschein: Spiegel der Indianer Seele

des homo primitivo

Vistas: Vistas und der einprägsame Ort

des besondere Ort, de

Aufmerksamkeit verdient

STEPHAN MARIA LANG

ARCHITEKTUR FÜR DIE SEELE

ARCHITECTURE – A JOURNEY TO THE SOUL

HIRMER

INHALT

CONTENTS

Vorwort
Foreword

Wenn man sich wahrhaft überlegen muss, „Wie möchte ich bauen?", so ist das nicht in zwei, drei Worten zu beantworten, sondern es bedarf Ruhe und Zeit, sein Vorstellungsvermögen zu aktivieren. Man muss sich darüber klar werden, was brauche ich, um mich wohl zu fühlen; welche Bedürfnisse beschäftigen mich, oder welche Sehnsüchte und Erinnerungen schlummern in mir, die ich in meinem Traumhaus umsetzen möchte. Architektur wird, wenn man sie oberflächlich betrachtet, gern kategorisiert in alt und neu, in modern und klassisch und in schön oder hässlich. Die Ursprünglichkeit der Architektur hängt aber mit den Menschen zusammen, die sich an ein Bauvorhaben gewagt haben, um ihre Wohnvorstellung mit einem Wegbegleiter zu realisieren.

Der Architekt als intuitiver Partner ist gefordert, das Gefühl für das Wohnen, das jeder in sich trägt, herauszuarbeiten. Es sollte gelingen, dem Bauherren die vielfältigen Gestaltungsmöglichkeiten vor Augen zu führen, um eine grüne Fläche zu einem visionären Raum mit allen Wunscherfüllungen in ein bewohnbares Gebäude zu verwandeln.

Meiner bemerkenswerten Bauherrschaft möchte ich dafür danken, dass sie mir das Vertrauen entgegengebracht hat, mit ihr das spannende Suchen und Finden ihrer Wohnvorstellung umzusetzen. Ich freue mich, dass sie ihre Häuser zur Verwirklichung dieses Buches Architektur für die Seele geöffnet haben.

If you truly wish to reflect on how you would like to build a house, this question cannot be answered in two or three words but requires tranquility and time to awaken your imagination. You have to be clear about what you require in order to feel comfortable, what your needs truly are and which dormant desires and memories you would like to integrate into your ideal home. Those who regard architecture superficially like to categorize it as old or new, modern or classical, beautiful or ugly. But the originality of architecture always depends on the people who have dared to go on a journey with an architect, starting from an idea and progressing through the building process, to transform their dreams into reality.

The architect, as the intuitive partner, guides the clients through diverse design possibilities. Through the fulfillment of wishes, he transforms the visionary space of a green site into an inhabitable, comfortable masterpiece of architecture.

I would like to thank my open-minded clients for having shown faith in my work, and for having opened their homes in order to make this book, Architecture – A Journey to the Soul, possible.

Stephan Maria Lang

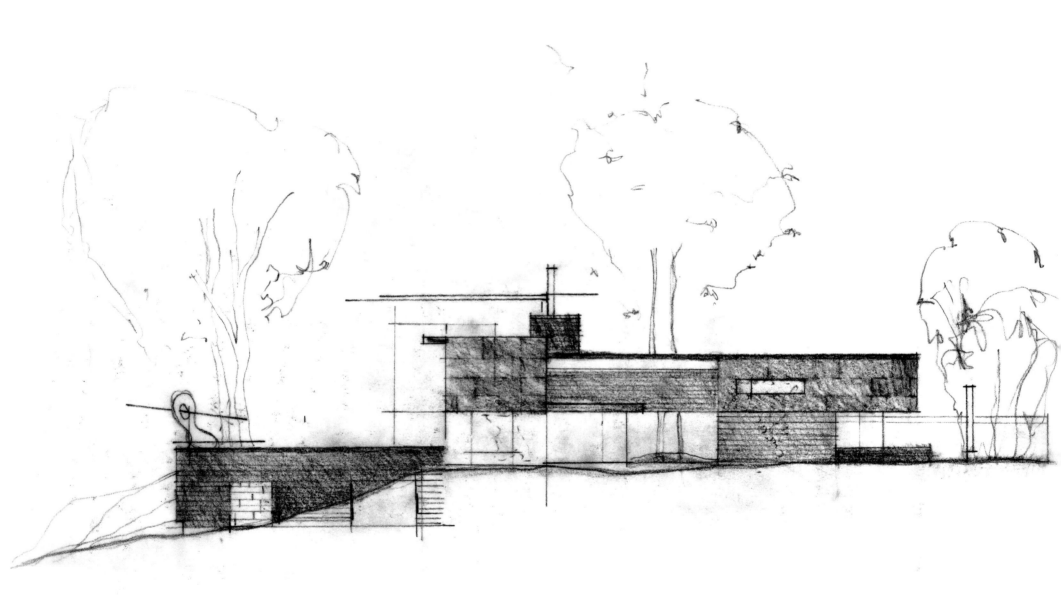

Einleitung
Introduction

Harry Dirrigl

Der Architekt Stephan Maria Lang besitzt die
außergewöhnliche Gabe, sich auf die Besonderheit
eines jeweiligen Ortes einzulassen und sie mit der
Persönlichkeit seiner Bauherren zu verbinden.
Dieses Buch illustriert mit einer stimmungsvollen
Bildkomposition die Vielfalt und Individualität
seines Schaffens.

Qualität und Schönheit in den Arbeiten von
Stephan Maria Lang liegen in den versteckten Details,
in den überraschenden Durchblicken, im Spiel von Licht
und Schatten und in der Integration von Landschaft,
Garten und Interieur zu einem Gesamtkunstwerk.

Der Band präsentiert mit sechs ausgewählten
Projekten, die zwischen 2004 und 2011 realisiert
wurden, die Vielschichtigkeit seiner faszinierenden
Architektur. Der Einsatz neuester Technologien ist
selbstverständlich, um dem Bedürfnis nach Komfort
und Energieeffizienz zu entsprechen. Wesentlich für
das Lebensgefühl sind jedoch seine Inspirationen aus
dem japanischen Denken, die Wertschätzung einer
Patina und die Schönheit des Unvollkommenen.

The architect Stephan Maria Lang possesses an
extraordinary talent for grasping the special quality
of any given site and combining it with the personality
of his clients. This book, with its atmospheric visual
composition, illustrates the diversity and individuality
of his work.

The quality and beauty of Stephan Maria Lang's
works lie in the hidden details, in the surprising
views, in the play of light and shadow, and in the
integration of landscape, garden, and interior into
a gesamtkunstwerk, an integrated and holistic
masterpiece of architecture.

This volume presents six selected projects, built
between 2004 and 2011, that reveal the complexity
of his fascinating architecture. The use of the latest
technologies is a matter of course in order to meet
the need for comfort and energy efficiency. However,
the essential qualities of this way of life are inspiration
from Japanese thought, an appreciation of patina, and
the beauty of the imperfect.

INTUITION

"IMAGINATION IS MORE IMPORTANT THAN KNOWLEDGE, BECAUSE
KNOWLEDGE IS LIMITED." ALBERT EINSTEIN

Haus P: geheimnisvoll, individuell, zeitlos
House P: Mysterious, Individual, Timeless

Dr. Oliver Herwig

O. Herwig: Herr Lang, wir sitzen hier am See, dem Starnberger See, an dessen Ufer viele Ihrer Arbeiten entstanden. Wo und wann haben Sie eigentlich die besten Gedanken für Architektur? Am See, am Morgen ...

S. M. Lang: Nein, weder noch. Eher beim Machen selbst. Beim Zeichnen. Wenn ich die Skizzen anfange, lässt es mich nicht mehr los. Wie ein Perpetuum mobile. Ich kann stundenlang grübeln, und irgendwann löst sich alles auf, und es geht weiter. Das passiert meistens direkt am Plan. Das sind die magischen Momente.

O. Herwig: Können Sie diese Augenblicke näher erläutern - was ging ihnen voraus?

S. M. Lang: Schwierige Dinge können dauern, manchmal zwei, drei Monate. Manchmal bleibt ein Detail unlösbar, dann stimmt im schlimmsten Fall das ganze Projekt nicht mehr. Und manchmal fließt es. Man merkt, wenn man den Kern getroffen hat, dann fügen sich alle Teile zusammen.

O. Herwig: Mr. Lang, we are sitting here by Lake Starnberg, on whose shores many of your works have been built. Where and when do you get your best ideas for architecture? By the lake, or in the morning, or ... ?

S. M. Lang: No, neither nor. More in the process of working. While drawing. Once I start with the sketches, it grips me. It's like a perpetual motion machine. I can brood over something for hours, and at some point everything is resolved, and it continues. That usually happens while I'm working on the plan. Those are the magical moments.

O. Herwig: Can you explain these moments in more detail? What precedes them?

S. M. Lang: Difficult things can take time, sometimes two or three months. Sometimes a detail cannot be worked out, and then, in the worst case, the whole project no longer works. And sometimes it flows. You notice when you have gotten to the core, then all the parts come together.

Leidenschaft für das Gesamtkunstwerk: für Detail, Haus, Interieur, Garten und Skulptur

Passion for the Gesamtkunstwerk: For the Details, the House, the Interior, the Garden, and Sculpture

Still liegt er da, der See, gerahmt von mächtigen Buchen. Ein Weg mäandert zum Ufer, verschwindet immer wieder zwischen Büschen und Zweigen. Wie ein Vogel hat die Villa Platz genommen über dem Wasser, an einem markanten Aussichtspunkt.

Wer sich dem Haus nähert, ahnt von all dem zunächst einmal – nichts. Ein Tor fährt auf, ein Vorhof öffnet sich und zugleich eine großzügige Vorfahrt.

The lake lies there, calm, framed by mighty beeches. A path meanders to the shore, disappearing now and again between the bushes and branches. Like a bird, the villa perches above the water, at a striking vantage point. Anyone approaching the house will not suspect any of this initially. A gate opens and a front yard appears, along with a generous driveway.

Detail – Hauseingangstür

Detail of front door

Kunsthandwerk: jenseits der Grenzen einer Serienfertigung
Artisanship: Beyond the Limits of Mass Production

Manchmal reicht es nicht über einzelne Bestandteile des Bauens zu reden, als wären es Teile eines wohl-dosierten Rezepts für Wohnkultur. Gute Erschließungen, angenehme Proportionen, ausgewählte Materialien und feine Detaillösungen sind hier selbstverständlich. Sie bilden die Basis für alles Folgende. Denn jeder sucht das Besondere, etwas, das ein Haus zu einem Heim und zu einem Spiegel der Besitzer macht.

Sometimes it doesn't suffice to talk about the individual components of the building as if they were part of a well-measured recipe for domestic culture. Good access, pleasing proportions, well-chosen materials, and subtle solutions to details are all a matter of course here. They provide the foundation for everything that follows, since everyone is searching for something special, something that will make the house a home and a mirror of its owner.

Modulation von Enge und Weite
The Modulation of Proximity and Distance

Was leicht wirkt, kann sehr schwer werden, und was auf den ersten Blick nach einer spontanen Eingebung aussieht, ist ziemlich sicher das Ergebnis harter Arbeit. Die Kunst besteht darin, all den Schweiß, die Mühen und Probleme beim Bau vergessen zu machen, sobald das Haus steht.

That which seems easy can be difficult, and what seems at first glance to be have been spontaneous inspiration is almost certainly the result of hard work. The art of architecture makes one forget the sweat, efforts and problems as soon as the building is finished.

Organische Einbindung
Organic Integration

Intuition ist die Fähigkeit, das Naheliegende gegen das scheinbar Abseitige einzutauschen und einen überraschenden Schritt zu tun. Es ist bestimmt kein Zufall, dass Stephan Maria Lang seit jeher Ambivalenzen faszinieren, mehr noch, dass er den Wurzeln seiner Arbeit nachgeht. „Ich bin verrückt und kompromisslos", ist so ein Satz, den er plötzlich in den Raum wirft, als wollte er nur die Reaktion seines Gegenübers testen. Und dann fügt er ganz ernst hinzu: „Ich bin jemand, der aus einer Türklinke ein Haus formt und darüber den Überblick verlieren kann." Dafür habe er seine Mitarbeiter, Spezialisten, die besser seien als er.

Intuition is the ability to exchange the obvious for the seemingly remote, and to take a surprising step. It is certainly no coincidence that Stephan Maria Lang has long been fascinated by ambiguities and that, furthermore, he explores the roots of his work. "I am completely crazy and uncompromising" is the sort of thing he will suddenly declare, as if he merely wants to test the listener's reaction. And then he adds quite seriously: "I am someone who forms a house based on a door handle, and can sometimes lose sight of the big picture in the process." To counter that, he has his coworkers, specialists who he says are better than he is.

3

Von der Seele schöpfen
Creating from the Soul

^{1,2} **Bootshaus mit transluzenter
Segeltuchhülle**
³ **Steg mit Badeplattform**

^{1,2} Boathouse with translucent
canvas cover
³ Wooden walkway with
swimming platform

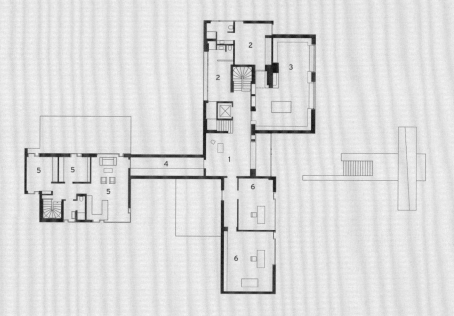

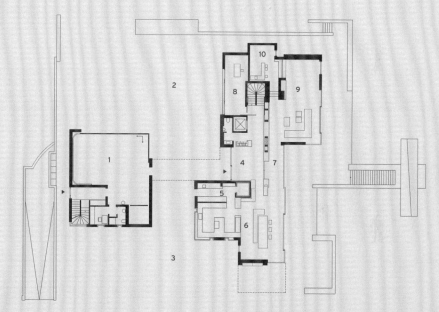

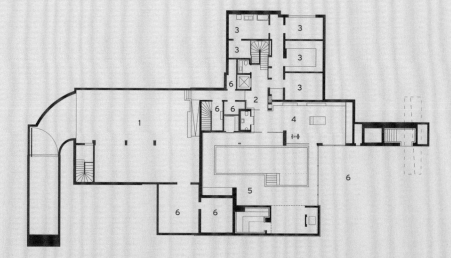

DIALOGUE

TIMELESS TRANQUILITY

Haus I: entspannte Moderne
House I: Relaxed Modernism

O. Herwig: Bauen, das bedeutet immer Dialog, Zwiegespräche zwischen Bauherr und Architekt. Brauchen Sie starke Dialogpartner, die Sie herausfordern?

S. M. Lang: Stark sind Bauherren dann, wenn sie im Prozess mitgehen. Wenn sie gespannt sind, was ich sage, und wenn sie auch darauf achten, dass der Architekt auf den richtigen Weg kommt, indem sie selbst dazu beitragen.

O. Herwig: Und wie soll das gehen? Sie sind doch der Architekt.

S. M. Lang: Starke Bauherren sind kultiviert und bereit, sich mit Architektur auseinanderzusetzen. Sie verstehen, dass ihre Entschlüsse Konsequenzen haben. Mein Ansatz erschöpft sich ja nicht, mit einer formalen Lösung aufzuwarten, sondern einen Prozess zu beginnen. Sie sind gespannt, wie es aussehen mag, und ich weiß es auch noch nicht.

O. Herwig: Building always means dialogue, a conversation between client and architect. Do you need strong interlocutors who will challenge you?

S. M. Lang: Strong clients are those who actively follow the process. Those who are eager to hear what I say, and who contribute to the architect finding the right way by participating in the dialogue.

O. Herwig: And how is that supposed to work? After all, you are the architect.

S. M. Lang: Strong clients are cultured and prepared to engage with architecture. They understand that their decisions have consequences. My part is not limited to offering up a formal solution, but rather involves starting a process. They are eager to see what it will look like, but I don't know myself yet, either.

Zurücknehmen und Hinspüren
Withdrawing and Feeling One's Way

Das Haus tritt von der Straße zurück, wortwörtlich.
Es eröffnet Raum, öffentlichen Raum mit wiegenden
Gräsern und Kiefern, die vor dem lang gezogenen
Rechteck des Gebäudes wie Teile eines japanischen
Holzschnitts wirken.

The building literally pulls back from the street. It opens
up space, public space with swaying grass and pines.
Against the elongated rectangle of the building, they
resemble sections of a Japanese woodcut.

Offenheit und Geborgenheit
Openness and Privacy

Weißer Putz, dunkles Tor. Und noch eine Schleuse, recht klein, damit der Raum dahinter umso größer wirkt. Hier wandert der Blick bereits in den Garten, dessen Büsche dazu aufzufordern scheinen, in den breiten Fensterlaibungen Platz zu nehmen.

White plaster, dark gate. And there is a channel, which is quite small, so that the space behind it looks that much larger. The gaze is already drawn towards the garden, where the bushes seem to call on us to take a seat between the broad window jambs.

1, 2 **Details Küchengarten**
3 **Überdeckter Sitzplatz**

1, 2 Details of kitchen garden
3 Covered seating area

Innen und außen
Inside and Outside

An der Grenze von innen und außen schöpft das Haus seine Kraft. Selbst der Küchentisch findet seine Entsprechung in einer zweiten Tafel auf der schattigen Terrasse, geborgen unter dem auskragenden Balkon. Vom Garten aus betrachtet, steht da kein einziges Haus, eher eine Komposition von Kuben, Vor- und Rücksprüngen, Volumen und Leerräumen.

The house derives its power from the boundary between inside and outside. Even the kitchen table has its counterpart in a second table on the shady terrace, hidden beneath a projecting balcony. Seen from the garden, this is not a single building but rather a composition of cubes, projections and alcoves, volumes and voids.

Der Architekt als Dienstleister
The Architect as Sensitive Craftsman

Sich selbst beschreibt Lang als Dienstleister. „Ich kann gut damit umgehen, wenn der Bauherr anderer Meinung ist als ich", schmunzelt ein entspannter Architekt. „Wenn er da oder dort noch ein Fenster haben will, dann fange ich nicht an zu streiten. Ich nehme es auf als bereichernde Idee, als spielerischen neuen Anreiz und mache etwas daraus." Der Perserteppich soll ebenso seinen Platz haben wie heiß geliebte Erbstücke, der Barockschrank oder das großformatige Bild.

Lang describes himself as a sensitive craftsman. "I have no problem with it when the client disagrees with me," says the relaxed architect as he smiles. "If he wants to have another window here or there, I don't get into a debate about it. I accept it as an enriching idea, as a new, playful stimulus, and I do something with it." A Persian carpet should have its place, in the same way that much-loved heirlooms such as a Baroque wardrobe or a large-format painting should.

¹ Detail Sitzstein
² Freisitz
³ Pool

¹ Detail of stone bench
² Outdoor seating
³ Pool

Lang sieht sich als Katalysator, dessen Ideen
Veränderungen beschleunigen. Letztlich, meint er,
gehe es ihm nur darum, seine Auftraggeber
„glücklich zu machen". Und das sei bei hohen
Bausummen mitunter schwieriger als mit geringen
Budgets. Das sagt Lang, weil er weiß, dass seine
Aufgabe nicht darin besteht, in endlosen Bemusterungen
Alternative um Alternative vorzulegen, sondern darin,
das richtige Stück zur richtigen Zeit zu präsentieren.
Das versteht der Münchner unter sanfter Führung.

Lang sees himself as a catalyst whose ideas accelerate
changes. After all, he says, all he cares about is making
his client happy and content. And that can be harder to
achieve with higher construction costs than with low
budgets. Lang says that because he knows that his task
is not to present alternative after alternative in endless
samples, but rather to present the right piece at
the right time. This is the Munich-based architect's
definition of "gentle guidance".

Saunabereich

Sauna area

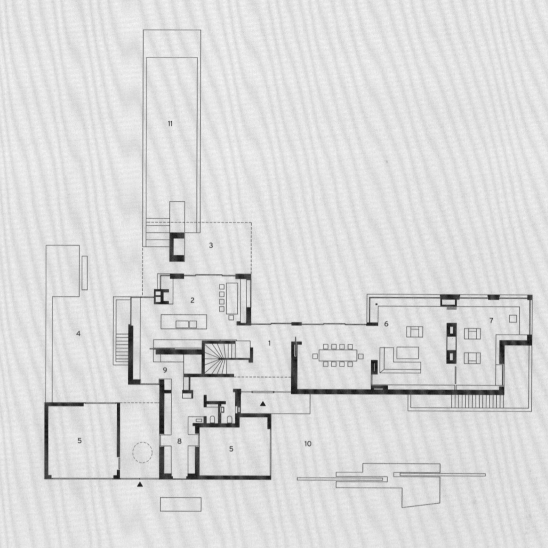

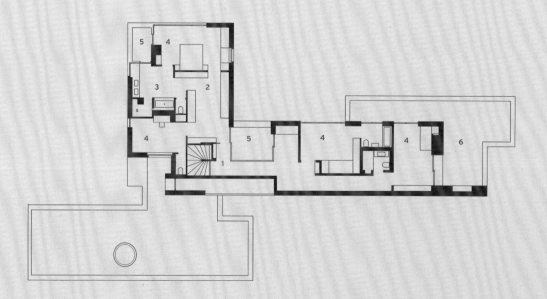

DETAILS

THE CRAFTSMANSHIP OF AN ARCHITECT

Haus G: Handwerkskunst im Detail
House G: Artisanship in the Details

O. Herwig: Jeder hochklassige Bau lebt von Details, von guten Lösungen, die womöglich perfekt ausgeführt wurden. Sie arbeiten seit Jahren mit einem halben Dutzend Handwerkern zusammen, die sie gewissermaßen an Ihre Standards herangeführt haben.

S. M. Lang: Mehr noch, es geht nicht nur um Qualitätsstandards, es geht um Übereinstimmungen, dass sie mit mir auf einer Welle sind. Mein Schlosser fährt zur Möbelmesse nach Mailand, ist Chillida-Fan, und wenn er mir eine kritische Frage stellt, weiß ich, dass das Detail nicht passt. Feingefühl ist ganz wichtig in der Zusammenarbeit.

O. Herwig: Every top-class building achieves its effect through its details and good solutions, implemented perfectly wherever possible. For years, you have been working with a half dozen artisans, whom you have, in a sense, raised to your standards.

S. M. Lang: Even more than that, since it is not just about standards of quality. It is about team work, the fact that we are on the same wavelength. My metalworker travels to the furniture fair in Milan, is a Chillida fan, and when he asks me a critical question, it shows me that one of the details might not be right. Sensitivity is very important when collaborating.

Holz setzt die Akzente
Wood Sets the Tone

Wahrscheinlich sollte man gar nicht so sehr auf das außergewöhnliche Flugdach abheben, das dieses Haus krönt, auf seine kubische Natur, die Tatsache, dass Glas hier Stein zu tragen scheint und unseren Blick umkehrt, oder auf den Schwimmteich, der als Reflexionsfläche dient und in dem sich Teile des Gebäudes spiegelnd verdoppeln, sondern auf seine verborgenen Qualitäten: Genauigkeit im Kleinen, Leidenschaft für Proportionen, seine handwerkliche Natur.

Perhaps one should not overemphasize the extraordinary shed roof that crowns this house, its cubic nature or the fact that glass seems to be supporting stone, inverting our gaze, or the swimming pool, which serves as a reflective surface and mirrors parts of the building. It is better to point to its hidden qualities: the precision of detail, passion for proportions, and its artisanal nature.

Vom Künstlerehepaar Hartmann
und Paul gestaltete Schiebetüre
zum Entree

Sliding doors to the entry designed
by husband-and-wife artists
Hartmann and Paul

Integrierte Sonnen- und
Sichtschutz-Lamellen

Integrated slats to shade
from the sun and provide
privacy

Präzision und Hingabe
Precision and Dedication

Wer Luxus sagt, meint Details, kleine Besonderheiten. Sie sind die ultimative Differenzierung vom Durchschnitt, von Standards und Massenware. „Ich bin für die Wünsche meiner Bauherren durchs Fegefeuer gegangen", sagt Lang. „Darum wurde ich so gut in Details."

Vielleicht hat das etwas mit dem Werdegang von Stephan Maria Lang zu tun, seiner Bereitschaft, für Architektur auch zu leiden. „Im Studium konnte ich gar nicht sauber zeichnen", gibt er mit entwaffnender Offenheit zu, „habe aber dann den Willen entwickelt, richtig gut zu werden." Genau das verlangt er von seinen Handwerkern, einem eingespielten Team, das er von Baustelle zu Baustelle mitnimmt, wenn es der Auftraggeber zulässt.

The word "luxury" suggests details, small special features. They are the ultimate differentiation from the average, from standards and mass-produced products. "I have gone through purgatory to satisfy the desires of my clients," says Lang. "That is why I am so good at the details." Perhaps that has something to do with Stephan Maria Lang's career, with his willingness to suffer for his architecture. "As a student, I could not even produce clean drawings," he admits with disarming openness, "but then I developed the will to become really good." That is precisely what he demands of his craftsman, a well-coordinated team he takes with him from building site to building site, whenever the client permits it.

Seit die industrielle Revolution den gestaltenden Handwerker überrollte, driften Design und Handwerk auseinander. Was einst einen Urkontinent bildete, in dem Entwurf und Ausführung unmittelbar verbunden waren, charakterisiert längst zwei völlig unterschiedliche Berufe. Sicher bestehen Verbindungen, gemeinsame Stoffe und Verfahren, aber zwischen den Schollen blubbert es wie flüssiges Magma, nicht zuletzt deshalb, weil die Trennung der Professionen Verletzungen hinterlassen hat. Da gibt es gefühlte Gewinner und vermeintliche Verlierer. Hier strahlt der Star, dort schuftet der Zimmermann. 1887 bereits beklagte William Morris das Ende der tätigen Handwerker, ihre „Rolle als Hersteller von Gegenständen nach freiem Willen ist ausgespielt". Das stimmt längst nicht mehr. Das Handwerk hat eine erstaunliche Renaissance erfahren, auch aus den Erkenntnissen der Moderne, dass Serie und maschinelle Produktion nicht Perfektion bedeuten müssen – und schon gar nicht Glück.

Ever since the Industrial Revolution steamrolled the designer artisan, design and handcraft have been drifting apart. What once formed a single entity, where design and execution were closely connected, has long since been characterized by two completely different professions. Certainly there are connections, shared materials and methods, but there are also rifts and crevasses, not least because the separation of professions left wounds behind. There are those who feel they won, and others who supposedly lost. Here the star receives all the attention, there the carpenter slaves away. In 1887 William Morris was already lamenting the end of the active artisan: "their part of craftsmen, of makers of things by their own free will, is played out." That has long since ceased to be the case. The crafts have experienced an astonishing renaissance, in part based on the experience gained from modernism that serial and machine production do not necessarily mean perfection – much less happiness.

Innenraumplanung:
Schreinerwerkstätten Gerhard

Interior design by
Schreinerwerkstätten Gerhard

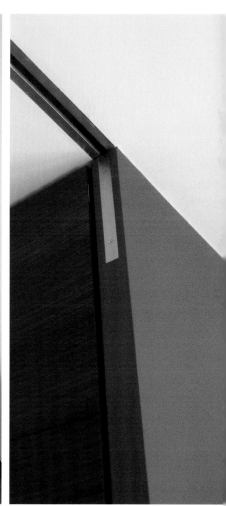

Hundertprozentiges gibt es nicht in diesem Leben. Lang spricht lieber von 98 Prozent und lächelt dabei so, als ob er an den restlichen zwei Prozent doch noch arbeitete. Details können einen guten Entwurf zu einem herausragenden machen – oder vollends verderben. Auf der Baustelle lässt Lang daher nicht locker. Man könnte das Sturheit nennen oder Perfektionismus; es bleibt der Wunsch, eine Setzung zu schaffen, etwas Bleibendes.

Nothing in life is one hundred percent. Lang prefers to speak of ninety-eight percent, and smiles as if he is still working on the last two percent. Details can turn a good design into an outstanding one – or completely ruin it. So Lang does not let up on the construction site. You can call that stubbornness or perfectionism; what remains is the design to set a standard, to create something enduring.

Detail Glasfassade
Detail of glass façade

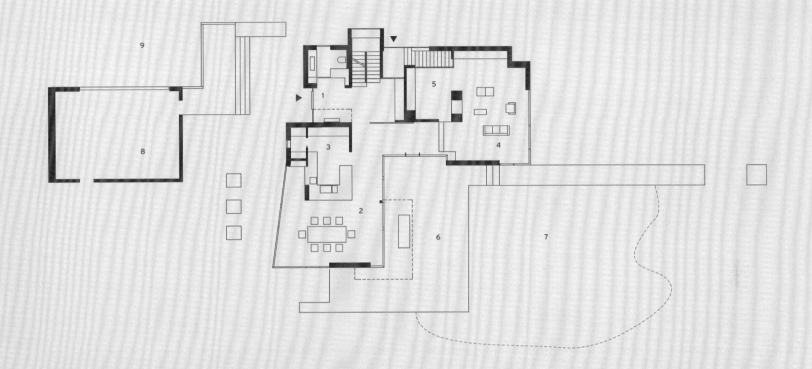

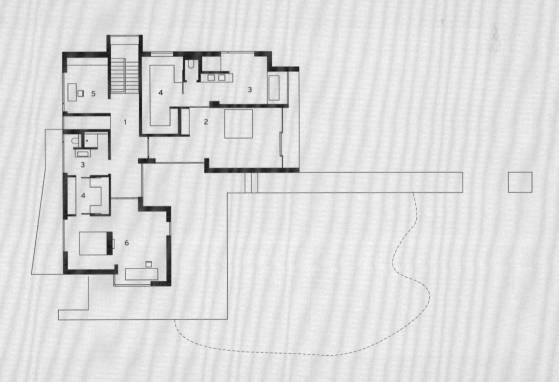

AESTHETICS

FOR YOUR EYES ONLY

¹ Haus S: Ansicht zur Straße
² Blick vom Arbeitszimmer
  in den Wohnbereich
³ Arbeitsplatz mit Seeblick

¹ House S: street view
² View of the living area,
  seen from the study
³ Writing desk with view of lake

Haus S: zeitlose Ästhetik
House S: A Timeless Aesthetic

O. Herwig: Ihren Ansatz haben Sie einmal als „Verfeinerung des Luxuriösen" umschrieben. Das ist ein durchaus ambivalenter Begriff. Wie meinen Sie das genau?

S. M. Lang: Ich habe kein Problem mit dem Begriff Luxus. Ein ambitionierter Schumacher möchte auch die besten Schuhe in der besten Qualität herstellen. Diese Schuhe halten ewig und sehen immer noch hervorragend aus. Ähnlich ist es bei Häusern. Wer sich ein Haus leisten möchte, das nicht in 20 Jahren wieder abgerissen werden muss, weil es womöglich ein Klassiker geworden ist, weil es gepflegt wird wie ein Bugatti und niemals langweilig wird, muss eben auch perfekte Materialien auswählen.

O. Herwig: You once described your approach as "refining the luxurious." That is a very ambiguous concept. What exactly do you mean by it?

S. M. Lang: I have no problem with the term "luxury." An ambitious shoemaker also wants to make the best shoes of the highest quality. Those shoes will last forever and still look outstanding. The same is true of buildings. Anyone who wants a building that does not have to be demolished again in twenty years, perhaps because it has become a classic, because it has been cared for like a Bugatti and never got boring, will have to select perfect materials as well.

Verfeinerung in Auswahl und Komposition der Materialien
Refinement in the Selection and Composition of Materials

O. Herwig: Verfeinerung läuft gemeinhin Richtung Purismus, Reduktion, Minimalismus. Sie besitzen diesen barocken Schaffensdrang, diese Lust am Mehr. Auch das hat ja was: Räume zu inszenieren.

S. M. Lang: Ein Haus muss inszeniert sein, auch wenn man darauf zugeht. Die Eingangssequenz wie in einem guten Film. Sie baut Spannung auf. Das räumliche Spiel kann nicht inszeniert und barock genug sein. Verfeinerung hat auch nicht unbedingt mit Minimalismus zu tun. Verfeinerung heißt einfach nur eine gewisse Reduktion in der Anzahl der Materialien, dass es nicht überladen wird. Es geht nicht um Sichtbeton und putzbündige Sockelleisten. Minimalismus ist eine reine Mode.

O. Herwig: "Refinement" generally moves in the direction of purism, reduction, minimalism. You have this baroque urge to create, this passion for more. There is something to that too: dramatizing spaces.

S. M. Lang: A house has to be dramatized, even as you are approaching it. An entry sequence as in a good film. It builds tension. The play with space can never be too dramatized or too baroque. Refinement does not necessarily having anything to do with minimalism. Refinement just means a certain reduction in the number of materials, so that it is not overloaded. It is not about exposed concrete and flush baseboards. Minimalism is pure fashion.

Stephan Maria Lang liebt keinen Stil, zumindest keinen einzigen. Wer länger mit Stephan Maria Lang spricht, gewinnt den Eindruck, er arbeite vor allem an einem: an genau komponierten Blickachsen. „Ich habe kein Problem damit, dass meine Häuser nicht modisch sind. Ich muss Häuser machen, die meinem Innersten entsprechen."

Das wäre die eine Seite, die des Künstlerarchitekten, der ganz aus sich schöpft. Die andere ist weitaus komplexer. Denn selbstverständlich geht es um den Dialog zwischen Bauherren und Baumeister, die sich im Laufe von Wochen und Monaten aufeinander einstimmen; Ideen, Wünsche und Vorlieben zu einem konkreten Objekt verdichten. Das ist keine Frage von richtig oder falsch, von Geschmack und Stil, eher von Haltung und Respekt.

Stephan Maria Lang does not love style, or at least not only one. Anyone who talks with Stephan Maria Lang for any period of time will get the impression that he works above all on one thing: precisely composed visual axes. "I have no problem with the fact that my buildings are not fashionable. But I have to create buildings that correspond to my deepest core."

That is one side: that of the artist-architect expressing himself. The other one is far more complex, for naturally it is about a dialogue between client and architect, who come to agree over the course of weeks and months on how to condense ideas, desires, and preferences into a coherent object. That is not a question of right or wrong, of taste and style, but rather one of attitude and respect.

Wohnküche mit Essbereich
und seeseitiger Terrasse

Open kitchen with terrace
facing lake

Tiefhof mit Wasserbecken
Water patio

Private Rückzugsräume
Private Spaces for Retreat

Da erhebt sich eine Mauer aus Naturstein über anderthalb Geschosse; doch statt Schwere auszustrahlen und Härte, ist sie filigran durchbrochen und hinterleuchtet wie ein Stück Stoff. Der geschützte Innenhof dahinter wird zum Rückzugsraum, zum Ort der Einkehr.

Das Perfekte verlangt nach Brechung, nach Perspektive, die das Glatte hinter sich lässt. Design sei in erster Linie ein gedanklicher Prozess, bei dem es um Inhalte gehe und nie um Äußerlichkeiten, meinte Dieter Rams einmal in einem Interview. Diese Maxime gilt für jeden, der Räume gestaltet und Leben zulässt.

A wall of natural stone rises up across one and a half floors, but, rather than exuding heaviness and hardness, it has filigree openwork and is lit from behind like a piece of fabric. The protected inner courtyard behind it becomes a space into which one can retreat, a place for contemplation.

The perfect demands refraction, a perspective that leaves the smooth behind. Design is first and foremost a thought process, which is about content and never about superficialities, Dieter Rams once said in an interview. This maxim is true for everyone who designs spaces and admits life.

^{1, 2} Bad zum Tiefhof
³ Schiebetürdetail: Griffmulde

^{1, 2} Bathroom facing water patio
³ Detail of sliding door:
    recessed grip

Entschleunigung
Slow Architecture

Stephan Maria Lang geht seinen eigenen Weg. Seine Wohnskulpturen wollen durchmessen sein, erlebt werden. „Wenn man alles auf den ersten Blick erfasst, wird es langweilig", sagt Alf Lechner, Stahlbildhauer aus Eichstätt und ein Fixpunkt in Langs Denken, das sich auffällig oft um Langsamkeit dreht, um Achtsamkeit. Um Atmosphären. „Und die Frage, wie sich dieser Anspruch in Architektur umsetzen lässt."

Stephan Maria Lang does things his own way. His inhabitable sculptures invite us to walk around and experience them. "If you can grasp everything at first glance, it will become boring," says Alf Lechner, a steel sculptor from Eichstätt and a fixed point in Lang's thinking, which strikingly often revolves around slowness, around attentiveness. Around atmospheres. "And the question how this ambition can be realized in architecture."

1 Aufgang zum Pool
2-4 Meer von Lampenputzergras und
Allium „Mount Everest" im Spiel
der Jahreszeiten

1 Steps leading to pool
2-4 Sea of foxtail fountain grass and
Mount Everest allium in the change
of seasons

Rhythmus und Perspektiven
Rhythm and Perspectives

Stephan Maria Lang dreht und wendet seine Entwürfe wie jene Skulpturen, die er aus Holz schafft. Und so entstehen sie wohl auch, als Rhythmen im Raum, offen für die Landschaft, die sie umfängt, mit gezielten Ausblicken. Das gelingt freilich nur, wenn die Fülle zuweilen auf Zurückhaltung trifft. Dann werden Blicke zurückgehalten und für das eine Panorama reserviert. „Ich gebe meinen Bauherren nicht Seeblick überall", sagt Lang ganz unvermittelt: „Es muss verschiedene Blicke geben."

Stephan Maria Lang turns and rotates his designs like the sculptures he builds from wood. And presumably that is how they emerge as well, as rhythms in space, open to the landscape that surrounds them, with calculated vistas. Admittedly, that only succeeds if the abundance sometimes meets with restraint. Then the views are held back and reserved for a panorama. "I do not offer my clients a view of the lake from everywhere," Lang says quite abruptly: "There have to be varied views."

Natürlich geht es um Funktionen, um Gebäude, in denen man sicher leben kann, um Türen, die sich öffnen, und Garagen, die Autos fassen. Doch kein Haus erschöpft sich im Nützlichen. Ein Haus muss unkompliziert sein. Es ist eine Hülle, eine weitere Haut seiner Bewohner. Dann arbeiten Architekt und Handwerker eben so lange an einer Treppe, bis ihre minimalistische Grundform durch einen kunstvoll gearbeiteten Lederhandlauf verfeinert wurde.

Naturally it is about function: about buildings in which one can live safely, about doors that open, and garages that hold cars. But no building is limited to functionality. A building has to be uncomplicated. It is a shell, a second skin for its occupants. The architect and the artisans work on a stairwell until its minimalist basic form is refined by an artfully worked leather handrail.

Hymne an die Horizontale
Hymn to the Horizontal

Haus am Hang, das ist eine Spezialität von Stephan Maria Lang. Dieses hier gleicht einer Hymne an die Horizontale, als ob sich hier schwebende Schichten aus Glas und weißem Putz angelagert hätten. Ein Haus für Segler, die kurz vor Anker gegangen sind, eine Art stilisierter Baumkuchen aus Balkonen, Terrassen, Ausblicken und Brüstungen.

Buildings on slopes are one of Stephan Maria Lang's specialties. This one is like a hymn to the horizontal, as if floating layers had formed from glass and white plaster. A house for yachtsmen and yachtswomen who have briefly dropped anchor, a kind of stylized layer cake of balconies, terraces, vistas, and parapets.

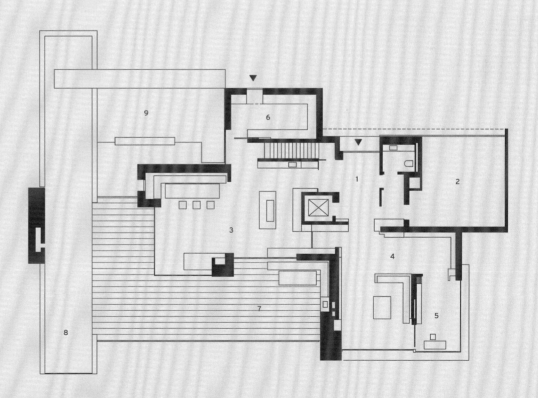

INTERACTION

HOUSE AND GARDEN

Haus T: die Verbindung von innen und außen
House T: The Connection of Inside and Outside

Eingangsbereich
Entrance area

O. Herwig: Wer durch Neubauviertel streift, hat nur allzu oft den Eindruck, dass für Gärten nichts übrig bleibt. Das Haus steht, da floss viel Energie und Liebe in die Wahl der Materialien und Möbel. Und dann stellt man fest, dass ja noch grüne Fläche rund herum existiert. Wie gehen Sie damit um?

S. M. Lang: In Absprache mit den Bauherren wird ein Teil des Budgets von Beginn an für die Gartengestaltung reserviert. Und selbst mit geringem Aufwand lässt sich viel Wirkung erzielen. Das Problem liegt ganz woanders. Für einen Pavillon im Park ist der Umraum egal. Aber unsere Grundstücke sind begrenzt. Wenn in der Mitte eine Schuhschachtel steht, entstehen zwei gute und zwei schlechte Seiten – und Resträume. Sobald sich aber das Gebäude wie eine Skulptur mit dem Garten verzahnt, gibt es unterschiedliche Gartenräume und spannende Aussichten.

O. Herwig: All too often, anyone wandering through a neighborhood of new buildings will get the impression that no attention is paid to gardens. The house stands there; lots of energy and love went into the choice of materials and furniture. And then one discovers that there is actually green space around it. How do you deal with that?

S. M. Lang: In consultation with the clients, part of the budget is reserved from the outset for garden design. And even without great expense, it is possible to achieve great effects. The problem lies somewhere else entirely. For a pavilion in the park, the surroundings don't matter. But our properties are limited. If you put a shoebox in the middle, you have two good sides and two bad ones – and leftover spaces. But as soon as the building dovetails with the garden like a sculpture, there are diverse garden spaces and exciting vistas.

O. Herwig: Was ist der häufigste Fehler, den
Sie beobachten?

S. M. Lang: Jeder Bauträger versteht unter Verzahnung
mit dem Garten drei große Glasscheiben. Und selbst
viele Bauherren stellen ihre Häuser wie auf einen
Suppenteller aus Terrassen, da weiß niemand mehr, wo
man nun den Schirm aufstellen soll, etwas mehr nach
links oder rechts? Neben der Terrassenwüste welken
Pflanzen als grüne Wurst am Zaun entlang. Es gibt
keine Orientierung, keine Blickachsen, Unangenehmes
ist nicht ausgeblendet ...

O. Herwig: What is the most common error you
come across?

S. M. Lang: Every developer understands "dovetailing
with the garden" to mean three large panes of glass.
And many clients too put their homes on a tray of
terraces, so no one knows any longer where to place
the umbrella, a little more to the left or to the right?
Next to the desert of terraces, the plants wither along
the fence like a green snake. There is no orientation,
no visual axis, no blocking of unpleasant sights ...

Raumerlebnisse schaffen
Creating Experiences of Space

O. Herwig: ... und was folgern Sie daraus?

S. M. Lang: Ich verstehe mich als ganzheitlichen Architekten, das heißt noch lange nicht, dass ich immer organische Formen bauen müsste. Ich kann Rechtecke bauen und die Natur trotzdem ins Haus hineinziehen. Mir geht es um erlebbare Gärten und Räume, in denen sich die Bewohner wohlfühlen, die aber auch höchsten ästhetischen Ansprüchen genügen.

O. Herwig: And what do you conclude from that?

S. M. Lang: I see myself as a holistic architect, but that does not by any means imply that I have to build organic forms. I can build rectangles and still bring nature into the building. I am concerned with gardens and spaces that can be experienced, that make the residents feel comfortable but at the same time meet the highest aesthetic standards.

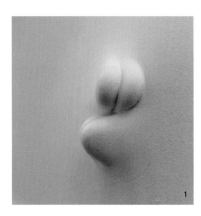

1 Gipskunst: Analia Segal
2 Blick nach oben aus dem Treppenraum

1 Plaster artwork: Analia Segal
2 View up from stairwell

Blick in den japanischen Gartenhof

View of the Japanese garden

Individuelle Gartenräume
Individual Garden Spaces

Wir sitzen in Stephan Maria Langs Mini und jagen über die Autobahn. Der Sommer brüllt, die Berge sind kaum mehr als ein feiner Dunsthauch am Horizont. Lang drückt sich den Hut in die Stirn, lässt das Schiebedach nach hinten fahren und sagt ganz unvermittelt: „Jetzt zeige ich Ihnen eine meiner größten Leidenschaften: Gärten." Die haben es dem Münchner Architekten angetan, seit er internationale Landschaftsgärten entdeckte, um für sich die Essenz daraus abzuleiten: Mut zur großen Geste. So stürmen Pflanzungen aus Lammputzergras und Rhododendren wie wild gewordenes Grün die Höhenzüge des Starnberger Sees, dort, wo Aussichtsplätze und großzügige Veranden stehen.

We are sitting in Stephan Maria Lang's Mini, racing along the autobahn. The summer is in full bloom; the mountains are little more than a delicate breath of steam on the horizon. Lang pulls his hat down onto his forehead, opens the sunroof, and says suddenly: "Now I will show you one of my greatest passions: gardens." The Munich-based architect has been taken by them ever since he discovered international landscape gardens and derived their essence for his own work: the courage to risk the grand gesture. For example, plantings of foxtail fountain grass and rhododendrons looking like greenery gone wild storm the hills around Lake Starnberg, a place of vantage points and generous verandas.

Präriegarten

Prairie garden

Geborgte Landschaft
Borrowed View

Inszenierte Gärten, die sich auf Schritt und Tritt
verändern, die nicht alles zugleich offenbaren,
sondern etwas zurückbehalten, etwas Entdeckerfreude
zulassen und doch klar und aufgeräumt wirken.
„Geborgte Landschaft" ist so ein Gedanke, den Lang
aus England übernommen hat. Er meint all das, was
in den Garten hineinragt, ihn verlängert und dehnt.
Deshalb legt der Architekt viel Wert auf die Ränder,
die Art und Weise, wie das Grün ausläuft, und ob Bäume
und Sträucher mit ihren Pendants jenseits der
Gartengrenzen harmonieren.

Orchestrated gardens which change with every step,
which do not reveal everything at once but reserve
something, permitting the little joys of discovery, and
yet seeming clear and cheerful. The "borrowed view"
is an idea Lang adopted from England. It refers to
everything that spills over into the garden, extending
and expanding it. That is why the architect places
such value on edges, on the way the green tapers,
and whether trees and shrubs harmonize with their
counterparts beyond the boundaries of the garden.

O. Herwig: Planen hat viel mit Intuition zu tun. Sie müssen sich auf andere Ideen einlassen, auf fremde Lebenswelten und Wünsche. Wie stellen Sie sich auf Bauherren ein?

S. M. Lang: Ich dominiere nicht; ich überrasche und verführe. Ich bin ein Katalysator, und wenn ich zuhöre, bin ich konzentriert. Ich stelle mich auf den anderen ein, erspüre, was er spürt, was er empfindet. Ich hole ihn da ab, wo seine Wünsche und Vorstellungen sind.

O. Herwig: Planning has a lot to do with intuition. You have to be open to other ideas, to the worlds and desires of others. How do you adapt to your clients?

S. M. Lang: I don't dominate; I surprise and seduce. I am a catalyst, and when I listen, I concentrate. I adapt to the other, sense what he senses, what he feels. I engage with him, with his wishes and ideas.

HARMONY

IN TUNE WITH NATURE

Haus K: Voralpenrefugium am See
House K: An Alpine Retreat on the Lake

Wie ein Spiegel liegt der Starnberger See da. Er scheint sich zu dehnen und lässt keine Grenzen zwischen Wasser und Himmel mehr erkennen. Ein Pfad führt zu einem Holzhaus, wie es scheint. Betonplatten, Kies und hohe Gräser. Der Weg wirkt unbenutzt, eingewachsen, als wäre er selbst schon Teil der Natur. Das Haus hingegen, mit seinen hölzernen Schindeln wie ein Schmetterlingspanzer über dem Betongerüst, ist beides zugleich: verwachsen mit dem Ort und doch spürbar anders mit seinem stilisierten Satteldach, wie eine jener nordischen Holzkirchen, die mitten in der Natur stehen.

Lake Starnberg lies there like a mirror. It seems to expand and to erase the boundaries between water and sky. A path leads to a wooden house, or so it appears. Concrete slabs, gravel, and tall grass. The path looks unused, overgrown, as if it too were already part of nature. By contrast, the house, with its wood shingles like butterfly armor over the concrete skeleton, is both at once: it has grown together with the place and yet it is palpably different, with its stylized gable roof, like those of Nordic wood churches, which stand in the middle of natural landscapes.

Stephan Maria Lang verharrt einen Moment, will schon etwas erklären und Dinge benennen, die Namen der Pflanzen liegen ihm auf der Zunge. Dann besinnt er sich und sagt gar nichts. Lässt den Ort wirken, das Haus selbst sprechen. Erst später, wir sind schon fast auf dem Rückweg, zeigt er auf die hohen Halme: Karl-Förster-Reitgras und Schneehäschen. An diesem Spätnachmittag am See wirkt alles stimmig wie eine Collage aus Wasser, Luft und Erde. Das Haus scheint hier schon immer zu stehen – oder zumindest schon sehr lange. Der Garten fließt ins Wasser wie der Steg ausfährt in den See.

Stephan Maria Lang pauses for a moment, wanting to explain something and identify things; the names of plants are on the tip of his tongue. Then he gathers his thoughts and says nothing. Allowing the place to have its effect and the house to speak for itself. Only later, when we are almost ready to head back, he points out the tall grasses: Karl Foerster reed grass and snowy woodrush. On this late afternoon by the lake, everything is as harmonious as a collage of water, air, and earth. The house seems to have been here forever, or at least for a very long time. The garden flows into the water like a footbridge into the lake.

O. Herwig: Ein großer Begriff, und darauf läuft das Buch auch zu: Harmonie. Einklang zwischen innen und außen, Mensch und Natur, Technik und Handwerk, Qualitätsansprüchen und eigenen Lebensvisionen. Reicht das? Ist damit Harmonie einigermaßen gut abgedeckt?

S. M. Lang: Was will man mehr? Wenn es dann noch gelingt, dem Ganzen eine spirituelle Komponente zu verleihen, hat man schon gewonnen. Heidegger meinte: Mit dem Wohnen erkenne man seinen Platz im Kosmos, mit dem Bauen gäbe man dem Idealen einen Ausdruck und mit dem Denken nähmen wir dies alles wahr. Schöner könnte man Harmonie nicht beschreiben. Wenn das auch nur annährend gelingt, wäre alles erreicht.

O. Herwig: One great concept, which is also central to the book: harmony. Inside and outside, humankind and nature, technology and craft in unison. Quality standards and one's own visions of life. Is that enough? Does that cover harmony reasonably well?

S. M. Lang: What more could one want? And if you also succeed in giving a spiritual component to the whole, you have already won. Heidegger wrote: By dwelling one recognizes one's place in the cosmos, by building one gives expression to one's ideals, and by thinking we perceive all this to be true. Harmony could not be described more beautifully. If one is even moderately successful at that, everything has been achieved.

119

Feuchtwiese

Natural meadow

Holzbearbeitung im Detail

Detail of woodwork

Harmonie und Brüche
Harmony and Rifts

O. Herwig: Trotzdem bauen Sie immer wieder Brüche ein, als wollten Sie Spannung aufrechterhalten.

S. M. Lang: Genau das umschreibt Harmonie. In Japan wird ein Hof erst blank gekehrt, um dann fünf Blätter wieder hineinzuwerfen, denn blank wäre er seelenlos.

O. Herwig: Even so, again and again you build in rifts, as if you wanted to maintain tension.

S. M. Lang: That is exactly what expresses harmony. In Japan, a courtyard is first swept clean, then five leaves are thrown into it, since it would be soulless if swept clean.

O. Herwig: Aber Harmonie braucht nicht immer einen Gegenpart in der Natur,
sie ließe sich auch in einer urbanen Landschaft herstellen ...

S. M. Lang: ... das weiß ich nicht, da wäre jedenfalls viel von meinem Anspruch, von
meinem Bauen verloren gegangen, weil ich Harmonie über die Natur zu erzielen
versuche. Ich will die Seele berühren. Harmonie in einem Industrieloft, mitten in einer
unwirklichen Gegend, das müsste schon ein sakraler Raum sein, fast eine Kirche.
Das Wohnen mit allen Sinnen, wenn man Himmel sehen möchte und Sterne, würde
schwierig. Aber mich reizen Schwierigkeiten. Nur, wenn man sie annimmt,
entsteht Neues.

O. Herwig: But harmony does not always require a counterpart in nature;
it could also be produced in an urban landscape ...

S. M. Lang: I don't know about that; in any case, a lot of my own ambition, of my way
of building, would be lost in the process, because I try to achieve harmony through
nature. I want to touch the soul. Harmony in an industrial loft, in the middle of an
unreal area, that would have to be a sacred space, almost a church. Dwelling with all
the senses, if you wanted to see the sky and the stars, would be difficult. But the
difficulties appeal to me. Only if you accept them will something new emerge.

Klangkörper für die Seele
Sound Box for the Soul

S. M. Lang: Mir geht es um eine durchdachte Ästhetik, die sich noch im kleinsten Detail ausdrückt. Um ein Gesamtkunstwerk. Nichts darf unnatürlich oder aufdringlich sein. Wenn ein Haus eine Schwingung ist für das eigene Ich und die umgebende Natur, kann das Haus nicht laut sein, sondern muss ein Klangkörper sein.

S. M. Lang: I am interested in a well-considered aesthetic that is expressed even in the tiniest detail. A gesamtkunstwerk. Nothing can be unnatural or obtrusive. If a house is to be a vibration for the self and for the natural landscape that surrounds it, the house cannot be loud but has to be a sound box.

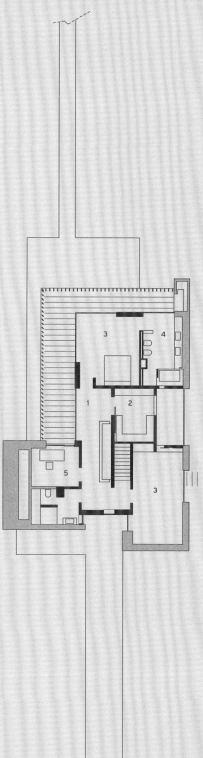

STUDIO

Holzskulpturen vor dem Eingang
zum Atelier
Wood sculptures in front of the
entrance to the studio

Atelier im Innenhof
Courtyard Studio

Ein langer Tag geht zu Ende. Der Mittlere Ring liegt
hinter uns, die Stadt umfängt mit sommerlicher Hitze
ihre Bewohner. Lang steuert durch einige Straßen
Giesings und parkt den Wagen im Hof des Büros.
Vor der Tür stehen Holzarbeiten, grob mit der
Motorsäge bearbeitete Holzstücke, die an Werke der
Konkreten Kunst erinnern, angereichert mit einem
Schuss afrikanischer Plastik. Daneben eine einfache
Biergartenbank und eine verwunschene Remise in
weichen Farben, halb eingewuchert. Ein Stück Land
mitten in der Stadt.

A long day comes to an end. Munich's ring road lies
behind us; the city surrounds its inhabitants with
summer heat. Lang drives through several streets
in the district of Giesing, and parks the car in the
courtyard of his office. In front of the door stand
artworks in wood: pieces of wood, roughly worked
with a power saw, that recall Concrete Art enriched
with a touch of African sculpture. Next to them a simple
beer-garden bench and an enchanted coach house in
soft colors, half overgrown. A bit of the countryside
in the middle of the city.

„Panta rhei – alles fließt"
"Panta rhei – everything flows"

Stephan Maria Lang ist das kreative Zentrum des Büros. Er benutzt seinen Computer, als wäre dieser ein elaborierter Farbstift. Der Architekt zeichnet, druckt Zwischenstände aus, collagiert und übermalt sie wieder, scannt neue Skizzen ein und bearbeitet sie weiter. Kreative Maßarbeit. Da öffnen sich Verbindungen, da werden Wege frei für Neues. Über 15 Häuser sind auf diesem Weg entstanden, im Schnitt eines pro Jahr, nicht viel, dafür Stück für Stück Maßanfertigungen.

Stephan Maria Lang is the creative center of the firm. He uses his computer as if it were an elaborate colored pencil. The architect sketches, describes interim states, makes collages and paints over them again, scans new sketches and then reworks them. Customized creative work. Connections open up, paths are freed up for something new. More than fifteen houses have been produced in this way, one a year on average – not a lot, but tailor-made, piece by piece.

STAND CLE

O. Herwig: Haben Sie eine Methode, Leerläufe zu überwinden und wieder in einen Flow zu kommen, wie Sportmediziner sagen?

S. M. Lang: Erfahrung. Sie hilft, nicht mehr zu lange an einem Problem zu sitzen. Die meiste Zeit jage ich auch nicht den genialischen Entwurf, sondern ein Stück Fortschritt. Man entdeckt etwas, und das reicht oft für einen ganzen Tag. Lieber nichts forcieren. Intuition lässt sich nicht erzwingen, manchmal fordert sie dazu auf, den Kopf erst frei zu machen. Ich pirsche mich immer wieder an, umwerbe manche Projekte wie eine schöne Frau. Und dann kommt der Durchbruch, dann entwickelt sich ein Projekt in wenigen Stunden.

O. Herwig: Do you have a method for overcoming unproductive phases and getting into the flow again, as sports physicians say?

S. M. Lang: Experience. It helps to keep you from sticking with one problem for too long. Most of the time, I am not chasing after a brilliant design but just trying to make a little progress. You discover something, and often that suffices for one day. Better not to force anything. Intuition cannot be compelled; sometimes it is necessary to clear your head first. I stalk again and again, courting some projects like a beautiful woman. And then the breakthrough comes, then the project evolves in just a few hours.

Der gemeinsame Weg
The Shared Path

O. Herwig: Sie materialisieren gerne geheime Träume. Wie geht denn das?

S. M. Lang: Wenn ich mich intuitiv hineingespürt habe, schaffe ich es, etwas Besonderes vorzuschlagen, und der Bauherr sagt dann womöglich: „Ich hätte es nie so beschreiben können." Aber das ist genau das, was ich will. Sich gemeinsam auf den Weg zu machen, ist das, was mich begeistert.

O. Herwig: You like to give secret dreams material form. How does one do that?

S. M. Lang: When I have felt my way into it intuitively, I manage to propose something special, and then perhaps the client says: "I would never have been able to describe it that way." But that is exactly what I want. Walking along the path together is what excites me.

LIST OF WORKS

GARDENS
LIST OF PRINCIPLE PROJECTS

GARDENS

"THOSE WHO WANT TO REALISE THEIR DREAM, HAVE TO BE WIDE
AWAKE AND DREAM MORE INTENSELY THAN OTHERS."
KARL FOERSTER

2007-8: Wandelgarten

2009: Kiesgarten

2009-10: Wald und Wiese

2011: Gräsergarten

2012: Steilhang

LIST OF PRINCIPLE PROJECTS

1999

House G, Kühbach

Collaborator: A. Lindermayer

Garden: H. Brugger

1999

Multiple Dwelling, Fürstenfeldbruck

Collaborators: M. Pfeiffer,
U. Binnberg, S. Reiss

1999

Virmani Shop Concept, Munich

Collaborators: B. Huber, S. Reiss,
U. Binnberg

2000

Semidetached House, Starnberg

Collaborators: S. Schwingenschlögel,
U. Binnberg, R. Meyer

Garden: H. Brugger

2000

**Reconstruction
ARAG-Versicherung,** Munich

Collaborators: S. Reiss, M. Pfeiffer,
U. Binnberg, D. Eberle, I. Werner

2001

Semidetached Houses, Munich

Collaborators: S. Reiss, I. Hornig

2001

Abendschein Lighting Design, Starnberg

Collaborator: J. Ingrisch

Color Concept: C. Nidhoff-Lang

2002

House F, Munich

Collaborators: A. Völkel, U. Walter

Garden: A. Koch

2002-3

Hotel Marina, Bernried

Collaborators: H. Kreye, U. Walter

Garden: H. Brugger

2003

Guido al Duomo Restaurant, Munich

Collaborator: A. Völkel

2004-7

House P, Ammersee

Collaborators: A. Hann, J. Noé, J. Rehberg,
S. Reiss, K. Schiffelholz

Garden: A. Koch

2005

House G, Starnberg

Collaborators: H. Kreye, S. Reiss

Garden: A. Koch

Color Concept: C. Hartmann, G. Paul

2005

Kabel Media, Showroom and Store Concept, Munich

Collaborator: L. Werner

Color Concept: C. Nidhoff-Lang

2005

Kindergarten, Starnberg

Collaborator: K. Schiffelholz

Color Concept: C. Nidhoff-Lang

2006

House B, Unterföhring

Collaborator: Engineering by client

2007

House M, Munich

Collaborator: J. Noé

Color Concept: C. Nidhoff-Lang

Garden: C. Bradley-Hole

2007

Expansion Guido al Duomo Restaurant, Munich

Collaborator: S. Hanft

2007-8

House M, Gröbenzell

Collaborators: S. Senula, A. Hann

Garden: A. Juhas-Barton, Design Associates – S. M. Lang

2008-9

House I, Munich

Collaborators: A. Hann, H. Kreye

Garden: G. Pape

2008-9

House T, Munich

Collaborators: A. Hann, T. Hofmann

Garden: A. Juhas-Barton, Design Associates – S. M. Lang

2009-10

House K, Seeshaupt

Collaborators: S. Senula, J. Charles

Garden: Design Associates – S. M. Lang, H. Köster

2010-11

House S, Starnberg

Collaborators: A. Hann, H. Kreye, K. Müller

Garden: Design Associates – S. M. Lang, H. Köster

2010-11

House W, Starnberg

Collaborators: A. Hann, K. Müller, T. Hofmann

Garden: Design Associates – S. M. Lang

2010-11

House D, Starnberg

Collaborators: A. Hann, K. Müller

Garden: Design Associates – S. M. Lang

ILLUSTRATION CREDITS

8-29 **HOUSE P**

Christopher Thomas: Pages 4, 12-19, 21-23.

Klaus Lipa: Pages 10, 24/25.

Hans Kreye: Pages 4, 8/9, 14, 26-28.

30-49 **HOUSE I**

Hans Kreye: Pages 32, 35-39, 40, 44-47.

Viewtopia_Bärbel Büchner, Christine Nidhoff-Lang: Pages 33, 34, 40, 41-43, 48.

50-67 **HOUSE G**

Angelo Kaunat: Pages 54-58, 60, 62-66.

Hans Kreye: Pages 50-53, 61.

Interior: Schreinerwerkstätten Gerhard with Siegfried Bruno Linke

68-91 **HOUSE S**

Hans Kreye: Pages 72, 75, 80, 81, 84, 85, 89.

Gordon Watkinson: Pages 68-71.

Marc Winkel-Blackmore: Pages 72-79, 81, 82/83, 86-88, 90.

92-109 **HOUSE T**

Walter Kirchner, Archiv Schattenplaner: Pages 94, 106-108.

Sebastian Kolm: Page 104.

Hans Kreye: Pages 92-94, 96-103.

110-131 **HOUSE K**

Walter Kirchner, Archiv Schattenplaner: Pages 124/125, 130.

Sebastian Kolm: Pages 124, 126-129.

Hans Kreye: Pages 110-116, 120, 121-122.

Viewtopia_Bärbel Büchner, Christine Nidhoff-Lang: Pages 117-119, 123.

132-143 **STUDIO**

Hans Kreye: Pages 132-143.

LANDSCAPE ARCHITECTS:

Koch&Koch Garten und Landschaftsarchitekten: Pages 14/15, 25, 28, 52, 54-56, 63-66.

Gabriella Pape, Königliche Gartenakademie: Pages 34/35, 37, 40.

DANK
ACKNOWLEDGMENTS

Ich möchte mich bei Harry und Petra Dirrigl,
Dr. Oliver Herwig und meiner Frau Christine Nidhoff-Lang
bedanken, die den gesamten Entstehungsprozess und die
Suche nach dem Ausdruck meiner Ideale begleitet haben.
Ganz besonderer Dank gilt meinen Mitarbeitern, die mit
Ihrer Leidenschaft und ihrem professionellen Engagement
maßgeblich zu meinem Erfolg als Architekt beigetragen
haben. Mein abschließender Dank gilt Thomas Zuhr
und dem Hirmer Verlag, die dieses Buch auf den Weg
gebracht haben.

I would like to thank Harry and Petra Dirrigl,
Dr. Oliver Herwig, and my wife, Christine Nidhoff Lang,
who have attended to the entire process of creating
this book and finding the expression of my ideals. I owe
a special thanks to my coworkers, whose passion and
professional commitment have contributed substantially
to my success as an architect. My final thanks goes out to
Thomas Zuhr and the publishing house Hirmer.

Stephan Maria Lang

IMPRESSUM
IMPRINT

Published by:
Hirmer Verlag
Nymphenburger Straße 84
80636 Munich

Edited by: Harry Dirrigl
Author: Dr. Oliver Herwig

Artistic advisor: Christine Nidhoff-Lang
Graphic design and typesetting: Petra Dirrigl
Hirmer project management: Rainer Arnold

Translation: Steven Lindberg
German copy-editing and proofreading: Alexander Langkals
English copy-editing and proofreading: Susanna Rachel Michael

Lithography: Repromayer Medienproduktion GmbH,
Reutlingen
Printing and binding: Aumüller Druck Regensburg
Paper: Galaxy Keramik 170 g/m²
Typeface: Anisette Std Petite, Interstate, Palatino

Printed in Germany

Bibliographic information published by the Deutsche
Nationalbibliothek. The Deutsche Nationalbibliothek lists
this publication in the Deutsche Nationalbibliografie;
detailed bibliographic data are available on the Internet
at http://dnb.d-nb.de.

© 2012 Hirmer Verlag, Munich, Stephan Maria Lang,
Oliver Herwig, Harry Dirrigl, Petra Dirrigl

Artist Rights: © 2012 Felix Weinold, Analia Segal, C. Hartmann, G. Paul

ISBN: 978-3-7774-5931-8 (German cover)
ISBN: 978-3-7774-5181-7 (English cover)

www.hirmerverlag.de
www.hirmerpublishers.com